Ronald
McNair

JUNIOR ■ WORLD ■ BIOGRAPHIES

A JUNIOR *BLACK AMERICANS OF ACHIEVEMENT* BOOK

Ronald McNair

DENA SHAW

CHELSEA JUNIORS

a division of CHELSEA HOUSE PUBLISHERS

FRONTISPIECE: *Ronald E. McNair, the United States's second African-American astronaut, stands beside a model of the space shuttle* Challenger.

Chelsea House Publishers

EDITORIAL DIRECTOR Richard Rennert
EXECUTIVE MANAGING EDITOR Karyn Gullen Browne
COPY CHIEF Robin James
PICTURE EDITOR Adrian G. Allen
ART DIRECTOR Robert Mitchell
MANUFACTURING DIRECTOR Gerald Levine

JUNIOR WORLD BIOGRAPHIES

SENIOR EDITOR Ann-Jeanette Campbell
SERIES DESIGN Marjorie Zaum

Staff for RONALD MCNAIR

EDITORIAL ASSISTANT Kelsey Goss
PICTURE RESEARCHER Sandy Jones
COVER ILLUSTRATION Gregory Baker

First Printing

1 3 5 7 9 8 6 4 2

Library of Congress Cataloging-in-Publication Data
Shaw, Dena.
   Ronald McNair / Dena Shaw.
     p. cm.—(Junior world biographies)
   Includes bibliographical references and index.
ISBN 0-7910-2110-6.
     0-7910-2116-5 (pbk.)
   1. Afro-American astronauts—United States—Biography—Juvenile literature. 2. Challenger (Spacecraft)—Accidents—Juvenile literature. [1. McNair, Ronald E., 1950–1986—Juvenile literature. 2. McNair, Ronald E., 1950–1986. 3. Astronauts. 4. Afro-Americans—Biography.] I. Title. II. Series.
TL789.85.M36S53 1994   94-2759
629.45'0092—dc20   CIP
[B]   AC

Contents

With Ronald McNair and six other passengers aboard, the space shuttle Challenger *stands ready for liftoff on the morning of January 28, 1986.*

1

A National Tragedy

The tragic final mission of the space shuttle *Challenger* on January 28, 1986, shocked the whole nation. Only 74 seconds after liftoff, the *Challenger* disappeared into a cloud of white, billowing smoke caused by a huge explosion that *engulfed* the entire shuttle. On television sets around the world, millions of people watched in horror as the 25th launch of the National Aeronautics and Space Administration (NASA) turned into a fiery nightmare before their eyes.

Although no one knew it at the time, the shuttle *Challenger* was in serious trouble even before it left the ground. Less than a second after takeoff, thick black smoke began escaping from a small open seal on the right solid rocket booster, one of the two reusable rockets that provide the power to launch the shuttle into *orbit*. The problem remained undetectable to the technicians at mission control, however, and preparations for the launch continued according to schedule.

"*Challenger,* go with throttle up," rang a voice from mission control as the shuttle's engines quickly reached full power. "Roger, go with throttle up," confirmed commander Dick Scobee from aboard the spacecraft.

All along the Florida coast, hundreds of family members, friends, and other well-wishers had braved the cold weather to witness the historic launch. The below-freezing temperatures were unusual for the Kennedy Space Center at Cape Canaveral, and the crowd of spectators bundled up against the cold and waited patiently to see the spectacular launch of the space shuttle. As *Challenger*'s rockets began to ignite, the crowd began cheering wildly in anticipation of the liftoff.

Less than a minute after takeoff, however, smoke and flames from the damaged rocket booster began to pour into the rest of the spacecraft. Within seconds, the fire ignited escaping liquid fuel, sparking a powerful explosion that destroyed the *Challenger*. The crew had separated from the rest of the spacecraft during the explosion. But without rockets to *propel* it farther into space, the cabin, with its crew members inside, fell back toward the waters of the Atlantic Ocean at a tremendous speed. None of the astronauts on board could have possibly survived the crash. In less than two minutes, the long-awaited flight of the *Challenger* was over, and back on the ground, the worst had been confirmed.

"It is with deep, heartfelt sorrow that I address you here this afternoon," announced space center director Jesse Moore, his voice trembling. "At 11:30 A.M. this morning, the space program experienced a national tragedy with the explosion of the space shuttle *Challenger* approximately a minute and a half after launch from here at Kennedy Space Center. I regret that I have to report that based on a very preliminary search of the ocean where *Challenger* impacted this morning—these searches have not revealed any evidence that the crew of *Challenger* survived."

What most of those who now mourned the *Challenger* crew did not realize was that the space shuttle's flight had almost been canceled that morning. After several weeks of delays, the engineers at Kennedy Space Center were concerned that the harsh weather conditions might have warranted yet another costly *postponement*. Freezing temperatures and rainy weather had settled for days along the normally warm, temperate Florida coast. During the night before the scheduled launch, temperatures had actually dipped to a chilly 27 degrees. By early morning, temperatures had risen to just above freezing, but the icicles that had formed during the night remained scattered on the scaffolding and equipment along the launchpad.

Some of the flight engineers were worried that ice might damage the shuttle's heat tiles during liftoff. Others warned that extremely cold temperatures might affect the seals on the solid rocket boosters. Since there had never before been a rocket launch in such cold weather, no one could predict with certainty what would happen if the launch proceeded according to schedule. At the last minute, however, the decision makers at NASA decided that the mission could proceed safely, and preparations for the launch were continued as planned.

Watching this terrible disaster unfold from the ground, the family and friends of the seven crew members stared at the sky in disbelief. Along with the rest of the spectators around the world, they were unaware of the concerns of mission control and were completely unprepared for the horrible sight taking place above them. They had come to share in their loved ones' great triumph.

Instead they had become firsthand witnesses to a shocking and tragic loss.

Among those present at the launch site were the family members of astronaut Ronald McNair. A 35-year-old scientist from Lake City, South Carolina, McNair had come a long way to find a seat aboard the *Challenger*. Growing up as an African American in a small southern town during the 1950s, McNair had to overcome numerous obstacles in order to realize his dream of becoming an astronaut, but, even as a child, he was always a fast learner and a fierce competitor. He excelled in athletics and in his studies, eventually earning a Ph.D. in physics from the prestigious Massachusetts Institute of Technology (MIT).

At the same time that McNair was completing his studies at MIT, the U.S. space program had begun an aggressive campaign to recruit *minority* astronauts. As one of the program's early minority participants, McNair trained at the Johnson Space Center in Houston, Texas, alongside a number of other African-American astronaut candidates.

There, he met Guion Stewart Bluford, the first black astronaut, and Colonel Frederick Gregory, a seasoned test pilot who received his earlier training at the U.S. Air Force Academy.

The January 28th mission was McNair's second flight on the *Challenger,* following his duties on the shuttle's successful first mission of February 1984. As a veteran astronaut, McNair was appointed as the crew's mission specialist, and his duties were central to the flight. He was in charge of sending a small, recoverable *satellite* into orbit. The device was designed to observe and photograph the flight of Halley's Comet through the earth's atmosphere. The most famous and magnificent of all comets, its flaming tail *illuminates* the earth's night sky only once every 76 years, and the fabled asteroid was already within sight when the crew began their final preparations for the *Challenger* mission. The United States was one of three nations planning to send satellites and *probes* to gather information on the famous comet.

Among the other crew members was Francis R. (Dick) Scobee, the spacecraft commander. Scobee was a nuclear engineer and a veteran of the Vietnam War from Cle Elum, Washington. At 46 years of age, this would have been his second trip

Christa McAuliffe (left) and Gregory Jarvis (center) were two of Ronald McNair's crewmates aboard the Challenger. *McNair is seated to the right.*

into space. His specialty was handling large, heavy aircraft. *Challenger*'s pilot, Michael J. Smith, was a 40-year-old native of Beaufort, North Carolina. Decorated as a navy pilot, Smith was making his first flight into space.

Judith A. Resnick, age 36, was *Challenger*'s flight engineer. A doctor of electrical engineering and a classical pianist from Akron, Ohio, Resnick was the second woman to travel into space, and this would be her second flight. Mission specialist Ellison S. Onizuka was a 39-year-old Hawaiian-born air force lieutenant. He was trained as an engineer and test pilot, and this was also his second flight into space.

There were also two civilian crew members on board the *Challenger*. Gregory B. Jarvis, a 41-year-old native of Detroit, Michigan, was chosen to work as a payload specialist and electrical engineer on the mission. Back home in Detroit, Jarvis was employed as a satellite designer for the Hughes Aircraft Company.

Sharon Christa McAuliffe was a 37-year-old schoolteacher from Concord, New Hampshire. McAuliffe had received a lot of attention from the national media when she was chosen from more than 11,000 applicants as NASA's "Teacher in Space" for the *Challenger* mission. Plans had been made for McAuliffe to conduct special lessons from space for schoolchildren across the United States. Each of the lessons were to have been filmed aboard the spacecraft and then later shown in schools. McAuliffe planned to call her first lesson, "The Ultimate Field Trip." It was to have included a guided tour of the spacecraft and astronauts' quarters and a detailed description of the crew's life in space. Her second lesson, "Where We've Been, Where We're Going, Why?" was to have traced the history of space travel, as well as NASA's plans for the future.

But the ill-fated mission of the *Challenger* and its crew would drastically alter the space program's future plans. What was meant to have begun a new stage in the celebrated program

Before his first spaceflight, McNair spent hundreds of hours training aboard the spacecraft simulators at NASA. These special rooms were designed to recreate life aboard a space shuttle.

resulted instead in the complete standstill of future space exploration. Following the disaster, President Ronald Reagan appointed a presidential commission to investigate the failed mission, and it would be more than two and a half years before another space shuttle would be launched with human passengers on board.

Meanwhile, people all across the United States mourned the tragic loss of the *Challenger* crew and the mission to which they had dedicated themselves. According to former astronaut Michael Collins, watching the disaster "was like witnessing a tiny, but vital, piece of this country being destroyed."

On January 31, three days after the tragedy, a memorial service was held for the crew at the Johnson Space Center in Houston. Among the more than 10,000 people who attended the service were President Reagan and his wife, Nancy. As the president spoke to those who had come to mourn, Nancy Reagan stood with her arm around Cheryl McNair, Ronald's wife.

"The sacrifice of your loved ones," said President Reagan to the family members who were present, "has stirred the soul of our nation, and through the pain, our hearts have been opened to a profound truth. We learned again that this America was built on heroism and noble sacrifice. It was built on men and women like our seven star voyagers, who answered a call beyond duty."

Two-year-old Ronald McNair (left) is pictured here with his brother Carl junior, age three. Raised in the small town of Lake City, South Carolina, both brothers demonstrated an early aptitude for learning.

2

A Studying House

Ronald Erwin McNair was born on October 21, 1950, in the small southern town of Lake City, South Carolina. The middle child of Pearl and Carl McNair, Ronald grew up in a home that emphasized learning. In addition to raising three sons, Pearl McNair taught school, while Ronald's father, Carl, worked as an automobile mechanic.

Both parents had worked hard all their lives to get ahead and were determined to see their children succeed. From the time he was a small child, Ronald was taught the value of hard work and study. Along with his two brothers, Eric and Carl junior, Ronald spent many hours reading the piles of books and encyclopedias that his parents brought home for the children. "Ours was a studying house," Pearl explained to a reporter years later.

Even before he started school, Ronald became known as a child who learned quickly. "The quality of his uniqueness showed up early," remembered his mother. "We always knew he was a bit different." By the age of three, Ronald had already learned to read. When Ronald was four, his father decided to send him to school a year early. "He was more than ready," explained Carl McNair, Sr. "I didn't see any sense in keeping him home." Ronald's love of learning would continue to be one of his greatest assets throughout his life.

Like most other southern cities during the 1950s, Lake City, South Carolina, was a *segregated* community throughout Ronald's childhood years. Black people and white people rarely interacted socially. Ronald's family lived among the other black families of Lake City, in a separate neighborhood from the city's white families. Separate schools and public places were established for whites and blacks.

Although Ronald must have felt the effects of segregation during his childhood, it seemed to have little effect on his attitude or behavior. "The segregated South did not affect us as deeply as it might have," explained Ronald's childhood friend Dozier Montgomery. "Though we lived in the Deep South, Ronald and I both had a parent who was a teacher. They sheltered their sons and were protective. So we weren't that conscious of problems."

At the age of nine, Ronald posed his first direct challenge to this segregated world when he tried to check out a stack of books from the Lake City Public Library. At the time, the library was a whites-only institution. "He decided to go to the library, and he refused to leave," remembered Pearl McNair. "The library workers called me. I rushed over and found police cars outside the building. Ron was sitting on the charge desk, holding a pile of books in his lap. His little legs hung down, not reaching the floor. I was pleased that he didn't want any trouble, just the books. He wanted to study."

Already, Ronald was on his way to making his mark on society. "From then on, Ron was allowed to borrow books from the library whenever he wished," his mother later proudly recalled. It would not be the last time that Ronald would enter an institution that had previously been reserved for whites.

Like many other boys his age, Ronald enjoyed all kinds of sports, especially baseball and football. Even on the playing fields, remembered Dozier Montgomery, Ronald always brought an intensity and sense of purpose with him. "Ron played," explained Montgomery, "but he was always serious."

When not studying or playing sports, Ronald was busy helping his parents and grandparents. "Ron always wanted to be doing something to help," recalled Pearl McNair. "He was very helpful in the house. In the kitchen, everywhere." Ronald was very close to his maternal grandparents, Jim and Mabel Montgomery. He spent hours of his free time assisting the older couple in their crate business. "Besides acting as delivery boy," said Pearl McNair, "Ron helped to keep the books." Ronald and his brothers also assisted their parents by spending their weekends and summer vacations in their father's automobile repair shop and doing other odd jobs to help with family expenses. "I taught my sons the auto body trade," explained Carl senior, "and [during] the summer months, they worked sunup to sundown picking cotton and beans, all for just $4 a day."

When news of the U.S. government's space research began to reach Lake City in the late 1950s, Ronald developed an early interest in the world of science and space exploration. Dozier Montgomery later remembered their frequent trips together to the neighborhood drug store.

"We bought comic books there," Montgomery explained. "Ron was also into science fiction. He always liked space books."

Ronald also stayed up to date on the advances in space exploration throughout the world. He read the newspaper stories excitedly on October 5, 1957, the day after the Soviet Union launched *Sputnik* (or, Fellow Traveler), the first artificial satellite to be sent into space. "I remember in elementary school when there was all this

Ronald's maternal grandparents, Mabel and Jim Montgomery, took pride in teaching their grandson how to handle responsibility. "As a youngster, he helped in his grandfather's business," remembered Ronald's mother. "He always wanted to be doing something."

talk about *Sputnik*," said Ronald's childhood classmate Rachel Scott. "That's all Ronald talked about—*Sputnik, Sputnik, Sputnik*. We got tired of hearing it."

On January 31, 1958, the United States matched the Soviet Union with the launch of its first satellite, *Explorer 1*. That same year, NASA was established to guide the U.S. space program.

In May of 1961, President John F. Kennedy challenged Americans to support the space program with a historic speech to the U.S. Congress. "I believe that this nation should commit itself to achieving the goal, before this decade is out, of landing a man on the moon and returning him safely to the earth," announced President Kennedy to the thunderous applause of the Congress. Following Kennedy's speech, the Apollo Moon Program was established to ensure that the United States—and not the Soviet Union—would be the first nation to reach the moon.

It was the Soviet Union, however, that made the next advance in the space program. In April

1961, the Soviet Union became the first nation to send a person into space when Yuri Gagarin, a 27-year-old *cosmonaut,* orbited the entire earth in 108 minutes—less than 2 hours.

"Trembling with excitement," recalled Gagarin in his memoir *Survival in Space,* "I watched a world so new and unknown to me, trying to see and remember everything. Astonishingly bright cold stars could be seen through the windows. They were still far away . . . but in orbit they seemed closer than the earth. But the point was not the distance . . . [it was] the principle. Man had overcome the force of the earth's gravity and gone out into space." Ronald McNair would one day see this same view from space.

Even with the Soviet Union's great advance, the United States was not far behind. On May 5, 1961, one month after Gagarin's historic flight, Alan B. Shepard became the first United States astronaut to be sent into orbit. By the mid-1960s, the two nations were both very close to reaching their ultimate goal of landing a human being on the moon.

Lake City, South Carolina, still seemed a long way from all the action taking place at NASA and with the Soviet space program. But Ronald's drive and dedication would eventually bring him closer to the space program than he would ever have dreamed possible. Even the seemingly insurmountable obstacle of Ronald's race would soon become unimportant. By the time Ronald was ready to become an astronaut, minorities had already begun to play a large part in the U.S. space program.

Accompanied by a federal marshal, James Meredith (right) challenged the racist segregation policies of U.S. higher education when he enrolled at the University of Mississippi in 1962.

CHAPTER

3

The Great
Lab Case

The United States Supreme Court declared segregation unconstitutional in 1954 in the historic
decision *Brown v. the Board of Education of
Topeka, Kansas.* It would be years, however, before most African Americans began to benefit
from the decision. For more than a decade, many
southern cities and towns continued to separate
black students from white students in open defi-
ance of the court ruling.

Like most other schools in South Carolina,
Carver High School remained segregated through-

out Ronald's high school years. As with most black schools in the South, Carver was poorly funded and able to offer its students little in the way of new books or supplies. Teachers had to provide their own educational materials, and, as a result, students received used supplies and out-of-date books from the white schools.

Despite the lack of proper materials, Ronald remembered his teachers at Carver as top rate. They stressed the importance of serious study and preparing for a college education. Young Ronald McNair was not the only student on whom the Carver faculty would leave its mark, however. "The Carver High School class of '67 produced quite a few teachers," remembered Ronald's friend Dozier Montgomery.

During his high school years, Ronald became more and more fascinated with the extraordinary ideas and inventions that he had first read about in the science fiction comic books at the neighborhood drugstore. Understandably, the young, would-be scientist was eager when he finally got the chance to try out his ideas in school. Though he immediately displayed an *aptitude* for science, Ronald's high school experiments were not always as flawless as his grade point average.

In one spectacular mishap that would later be known as the "great lab case," Ronald and his friend Archie Alford decided to perform an after-hours experiment in the Carver High School chemistry lab. The two had read in a textbook that a small explosion could be produced by mixing sodium and water. Disregarding the modest portions recommended in the book, the boys threw a large dose of sodium into a sink filled with water. A large explosion quickly filled the lab with thick black smoke, and the boys fled the building in terror. Luckily, the two escaped injury. When they were finally caught, remembered Dozier Montgomery, the school officials seemed more impressed with their resourcefulness than angry about the prank.

Even with his interest in scientific experiments, Ronald excelled in many other subjects.

"He was exceedingly bright, the class leader," recalled Carver economics teacher Harry Fleming. "His adrenaline never stopped flowing. He was always prodding his teachers to 'go faster,' even when you already thought you were going faster."

Ronald's enthusiasm and desire for perfection had a positive impact on his classmates. "We all knew that Ron was smarter than the rest of us," explained Lake City councilman, and Ronald's former classmate, Wilford Barr. "We all knew that he was going to get that 100 on a test. However, his determination made the rest of us eager to study hard to at least get a 99."

With his sterling record in the classroom, many people assumed that Ronald would be unable to compete physically with the other boys at sports. When McNair tried out for the high school football team, Coach Jack Williams eyed the lanky, bespectacled freshman with raised eyebrows. To the experienced coach, Ronald seemed more like the honor roll type than the sack-the-quarterback type.

But Ronald was always full of surprises. In typical McNair fashion, he gave the same 100 percent on the football field that he gave in the classroom. To the coach's amazement, Ronald quickly earned a spot as starting linebacker for the Carver Panthers. According to Coach Williams, Ronald proved to be "a total football player." "He was vicious," Williams recalled. "Anything Ronald set out to do, he did."

In addition to football, Ronald was also on the track and basketball teams and starred on the baseball diamond. "Whatever Ronald did, it had to be a challenge," said McNair's childhood friend Wallace Scott. "If it wasn't a challenge, Ronald just wouldn't bother with it."

At age 13, McNair demonstrates his basketball skills on the playground outside Carver High School. The studious youngster impressed his coaches and teammates with his athletic ability.

One of Ronald's favorite subjects was music. He played the saxophone in the Carver High School band and was serious enough about performing to think about majoring in music once he entered college. "Most people think Ron always played sax," explained Dozier Montgomery, "but the clarinet was his first love. Whatever [he played], he was good at it."

At the end of his senior year, Ronald was named *valedictorian* of Carver High School's class of 1967. Like many of his classmates, he was now faced with selecting a college. Fifty of Ron's 150 fellow graduates went on to pursue a higher education, a remarkable number for a black southern high school in the 1960s.

Most African-American students were limited in their choice of colleges and universities, as many schools had not yet opened their doors to black students. Officially, the battle for equal education had been won in 1962, when James Meredith successfully fought to attend the previously all-white University of Mississippi. A war veteran, Meredith obtained a federal court order to allow him to enter the university and was escorted to his classes by federal marshals after Mississippi governor Ross Barnett refused to honor the court's decision. Even after the Meredith incident, however, most southern colleges were reluctant to admit African-American students, and many young people had little choice but to attend regional black colleges.

Two hundred fifty thousand miles above Lake City, South Carolina, another struggle was taking place. Throughout the late 1960s, the United States and the Soviet Union continued their race into space. While the Russians launched spacecrafts to the moon with no astronauts on board, U.S. scientists busily prepared *Apollo 8* for its historic flight. Finally, on December 21, 1968, the first spaceship carrying human passengers began its 500,000-mile flight to the moon and back.

For the first time, people were able to see the whole earth from space. At such great heights, the planet appeared to the pioneers of *Apollo 8* as a tiny blue sphere floating in the black vastness of space. One astronaut described the earth as "the big blue marble." To crew member Frank Borman, the moon looked like "a vast, lonely, and forbidding planet."

Meanwhile, the Soviet Union continued to explore space from the earth's orbit. By July of 1969, it appeared that the United States had the moon all to itself. Just two years after Ronald graduated from high school, three astronauts—Neil Armstrong, Edwin Aldrin, and Michael Collins—would make history as the first crew to land on the moon. "Houston, *Tranquility* base here," came Armstrong's first words as he landed the lunar module on the moon. Later that day, Armstrong would become the first human being to set foot on the moon. "That's one small step for man," he said as he climbed down from the spacecraft and onto the lunar surface, "one giant leap for mankind."

Back in Lake City, Ronald and his brother Carl junior were preoccupied with less dramatic events. Both young men chose North Carolina Agricultural and Technical State University, known as Greensboro A&T, as their school of preference. The tiny North Carolina college was the best school in the area that openly accepted minorities. To their delight, both Ronald and Carl were admitted, with Ronald winning an academic *scholarship* for his outstanding achievements at Carver High School.

Greensboro A&T also specialized in science and engineering, the subjects in which both brothers would eventually major. Surprisingly, Ronald's first choice was to study music. Recognizing the young man's special aptitude for science, however, the guidance counselor at the college persuaded him to concentrate on physics. "I think you're good enough," the counselor encouraged him. The counselor's words gave Ronald the confidence to give the demanding field of science a try.

McNair spent his junior year of college as an exchange student at the prestigious Massachusetts Institute of Technology (MIT). Thrilled by the educational opportunities offered there, he was unprepared for its racial hostility.

4

Heading North

At Greensboro A&T, McNair encountered many new challenges that would put his academic excellence to the test. For the first time, he was competing with students from all over the country. Many of his classmates had received a more thorough education than he was able to receive from the poorly funded school system in Lake City. Although Carver High School's teachers did their best with the funds and resources that they had, they were not always able to offer their students a complete selection of subjects or up-to-date resources.

McNair worked hard to make up for what he had missed in high school. He spent many late nights in the college library and carried a book with him wherever he went. Before long, he was earning top grades in his course work, particularly in the science program.

In Greensboro, McNair abandoned the roughness of football for the graceful and powerful art of karate. Studying karate required intense discipline and concentration and offered Ronald a different kind of challenge. By the end of his first semester, his beginning karate class of 200 students had dwindled down to five. By the time he reached his senior year at A&T, he was the only remaining student in his karate class and had earned the sport's highest ranking, a fifth-degree black belt.

McNair would win many other honors. During his junior year, he was selected to participate in a North-South educational exchange program. As a gifted young black student, he was chosen to spend a year at the Massachusetts Institute of Technology (MIT) in Cambridge, Massachusetts. As one of the sponsors of the exchange program, the prestigious university hoped to bring more minorities into the fields of science and engineering.

In 1969, at the beginning of his junior year, McNair was excited to have the chance to discover what life was like in the northern part of the United States. Founded in 1961, MIT, one of the top universities in the country for science and engineering, was well known for its demanding classwork and excellence in education. "Even the janitors at MIT had masters degrees," Ronald later joked.

When McNair enrolled there in 1969, MIT had more than 7,500 students. Only 200 of those students were African Americans. While Ronald quickly excelled in the MIT physics department, he also encountered racial hostility on the campus and in the surrounding community. Just as in cities and towns throughout the South, the city of Cambridge also struggled with desegregating its communities and schools. Change came slowly there and in Boston, and black people were often the victims of threats and verbal hostility.

After leaving a karate class one day, McNair was surrounded by an angry gang of white men who threatened to harm him if he refused to leave MIT. With his skills in karate, Ronald stopped the attack and managed to escape unharmed. But such incidents caused the young scholar to question why he was studying at an institution where he faced danger and *ridicule* every day. Ronald did his best to ignore the *racism,* however, and concentrate on his studies. He had come to MIT because it was the best school he could find, and he was determined to get a good education, regardless of the *prejudice* around him.

The following year, McNair returned to Greensboro A&T, where he completed his bachelor's degree in physics in 1971. At graduation, Ronald was awarded the honor of magna cum

McNair began studying karate in college. By the end of
his senior year, he had achieved a fifth-degree black belt
and qualification as an instructor. Here he is pictured
with fellow student William Perry (right).

laude (the Latin words for great distinction). After his success as an undergraduate, he was eager to return to school to work toward his Ph.D. in physics.

Once again, McNair set his standards high. He chose and was accepted into the doctoral program in physics at MIT. But he still had his doubts about returning to the Boston area. "At first I wasn't going, but then I couldn't run away from a challenge," he explained. "I had to compete with the best."

Having been accepted by MIT, McNair still had to find a way to pay for his education. The prestigious university in Cambridge was among the most expensive educational institutions in the country. Following the advice of his college counselor, Tom Sandin, Ronald applied for a scholarship from the Ford Foundation, a large financial trust that often aided black students with proven intellectual abilities and leadership qualities. "If you can't give this fellowship to Ron McNair," wrote Sandin to the foundation's review committee, "you can't give it to anyone." Understandably, the Ford Foundation was impressed and McNair received the scholarship.

Back in Cambridge for the fall of 1971, McNair was once again forced to struggle against racial prejudice. "We all recognized the [uncertainty] of our positions in the country, in the city, and at the institution," remembered Gregory Chisholm, one of McNair's classmates from the period.

Also at MIT, McNair met classmates who had received undergraduate degrees from top universities around the nation, such as Harvard and Stanford. He discovered to his dismay that many of the students were better prepared than he was to meet the strenuous standards at MIT. As with everything else in his life, however, McNair was determined to succeed, even if it meant spending all of his time in the library. "Given McNair's fairly inadequate background," remembered Michael Feld, one of Ronald's advisers at MIT, "it took tremendous determination to bring himself up to speed. But he was able to muster that kind of resolve."

Working closely with his faculty advisers, McNair planned a course of study that would make up for any gaps in his education. He took courses in electrical engineering, advanced physics, and even a few undergraduate classes in order to make up for the courses that he had missed in the past. His hard work soon began to pay off, but not before he encountered some serious setbacks that could have *jeopardized* his future at the school.

As one of the requirements for a Ph.D. in physics, McNair and the other physics students were required to pass a five-hour qualifying exam. Ronald was terribly disappointed when he learned that he had failed the test. After studying again, however, he took the test a second time and passed with high marks.

McNair faced an even greater setback when he lost his scientific notebook filled with all of his experimental data. "That was two years worth of work," explained Michael Feld. "But Ronald never complained. He went back to work in the laboratory, and in a few months time the second set of data was complete, and it turned out better than the first data. That was typical of the way he worked to accomplish goals."

Toward the end of his studies, McNair specialized in laser research, a highly technical field that involves the pinpoint control of light beams and electricity. During his final years at MIT, he helped develop new laser technologies that would later be used in the U.S. space program. According to Michael Feld, McNair wrote a "very solid" doctoral thesis on laser physics, in addition to several impressive technical publications. After graduation, Ronald continued to publish papers and to lecture to scientific groups on the latest developments in laser research.

Though McNair had little free time at MIT, he continued to play his saxophone and develop his skills in karate. He even found time to teach a karate class for beginners at St. Paul's African

Episcopal Church in Cambridge. One night after class, he stayed late for a church-sponsored pot-luck supper. There he met Cheryl Moore, a school-teacher from Jamaica, New York. Ronald and Cheryl quickly developed a close relationship, and the two were married on June 27, 1976, in the same church building where they met.

Upon completion of his studies at MIT, McNair and his new wife headed west to Malibu, California, where he had accepted the position of staff physicist at Hughes Research Laboratories. One of the largest laser research facilities in the country, Hughes gave McNair the chance to put to practical use the skills and knowledge that he had acquired at MIT. Part of Ronald's new work involved research on lasers for communication between satellites in space. McNair soon developed a reputation for excellence at his new job, and his achievements began to gain attention outside of the Hughes facility.

Not long after he began working at Hughes Laboratories, McNair received a letter in the mail from NASA inviting him to apply to be an astronaut. The NASA space program had recently begun a drive to recruit gifted minority scientists, engineers, and pilots for the space program, and Ronald was among its most outstanding prospects. This was the chance that he had been waiting for, and he immediately applied. According to his mother, McNair was "calm and confident" that he would be chosen for a spot in the astronaut training program.

In January of 1978, McNair was chosen from among 10,000 applicants as one of 34 new recruits for the space program. Once again, he and Cheryl packed their bags to travel to a new home. This time they were heading east, to the Johnson Space Center in Houston, Texas.

McNair (left) and his fellow black astronauts-in-training pose for photographers in January 1978. To McNair's left is pilot Frederick D. Gregory, and seated is Guion Stewart Bluford, Jr., the first African American to be launched into space.

CHAPTER

5
Preparing
for Space

After the exciting space achievements of the late 1960s and early 1970s, NASA realized that a new type of spacecraft was needed in order for its missions to operate more *efficiently*. With plans for increased space travel in the 1980s, the one-way, disposable crafts that had been used in the past were simply too costly. In January 1972, NASA announced its plan to develop a "national space transportation system," or space shuttle. The shuttle would be a reusable aerospace craft designed to travel round-trip between earth and space. Unlike its *predecessors,* the same shuttle could be used for several launches.

"NASA engineers were intrigued by the idea of flying one vehicle over and over," explained astronaut Michael Collins. "It implied a techno-logical maturity, a feeling that space was here to stay. . . . For an aeronautical engineer, the path to reusability was glorious." According to Collins, the shuttle "would launch vertically, like its rocket predecessors, but fly back to a horizontal landing like a *conventional* airplane."

By 1981, engineers at NASA had completed four working space shuttles: the *Columbia,* the *Challenger,* the *Discovery,* and the *Atlantis.* On April 12 of that year, NASA successfully tested the first of these shuttles, the *Columbia.* Two years later, on April 4, 1983, the second shuttle, the *Challenger,* flew its first mission. Carrying a crew of four astronauts, the *Challenger* mission was a great success. Built lighter and stronger than the rest of the fleet, the *Challenger* became the most impressive vehicle of the U.S. space program.

McNair arrived in Houston in January 1978 to train as a mission specialist. He had a lot of work ahead of him. The training program was rigorous. Ronald and his classmates had a tough, around-the-clock schedule of study and preparation. Before completing the training program, they had to endure a series of demanding tests to prepare them for life above the earth's atmosphere. In addition to the physical training, each candidate signed up for a heavy load of course work. Ronald and his fellow students took classes in advanced mathematics, earth resources, meteorology, guidance and navigation, astronomy, and computer science.

Along with his academic studies, McNair was learning how to survive without the benefit of the earth's gravity to hold his feet on the ground. Once a spacecraft escapes the earth's atmosphere, the gravity that keeps earthbound people on the ground disappears. This can cause many problems for those who are not prepared. "You carry with you your own body-oriented world," explained one veteran astronaut, "in which up is over your head, down is below your feet, and you take this world around with you wherever you go." In space, however, there is nothing to stand on. There is literally no up or down, and astronauts are completely weightless. Being weightless feels like falling but never landing. Astronauts prepare for weightlessness by working underwater or flying in airplanes that fall freely for several seconds at a time.

One important skill that McNair and his fellow trainees learned was how to sleep in a weightless environment. Before going to sleep each night, astronauts strap themselves to their beds to keep from floating into the walls or one another. After they get used to the procedure, however, most astronauts report that sleeping in space is just as comfortable as sleeping on earth. Eating can also prove tricky in this atmosphere. Astronauts who move their forks too quickly often see their food go floating away across the cabin.

During his period of training, McNair also practiced working in special pressurized suits that would protect him from the environment of space outside the shuttle. The space suit had everything an astronaut needed in order to survive in space and was almost like a self-contained spacecraft. "A space flight begins," explained astronaut Michael Collins, "when the technician snaps your helmet down into your neck ring and locks it in place. From that moment on, no outside air will

During their training, NASA cadets spend many hours in simulated zero-gravity chambers. Here fledgling astronauts McNair and Rhea Seddon receive instruction in weightless maneuvering from an instructor during a 1979 exercise.

be breathed, only bottled oxygen; no human voice heard, unless electronically piped in through the barrier of the pressure suit. The world can still be seen, but that is all—not smelled, or heard, or felt, or tasted."

After six hard years of training, McNair was finally ready to begin his work as a mission specialist aboard a space shuttle. As he had with other challenges earlier in his life, McNair excelled at NASA, making whatever personal sacrifices were necessary to meet his own high standards. Fellow trainee Charles Bolden called Ron "an exceptional individual." "I don't think any one person could have kept up with Ron to know all the things that he was into," added Bolden admiringly. "He was absolutely phenomenal. He never had a normal time that was day or night. Ron did these things until they were finished, and if that meant going past midnight, then he did."

In 1982, toward the end of Ron's training at Houston, the McNairs had their first child, a boy they named Reginald. McNair would be a seasoned astronaut by the time Cheryl gave birth to their second child, a daughter named Joy Cheray, born on July 20, 1984.

In 1984, McNair finally received his first opportunity to travel into space. On February 3, at 8:00 P.M., the space shuttle *Challenger* blasted off successfully from Kennedy Space Center. The astronauts who accompanied McNair on Mission 41-B, as NASA called it, were scheduled to perform a number of tasks. As on the earlier space shuttle flights, their primary objectives included putting satellites into orbit around the earth and testing new equipment. But the second *Challenger* mission would also be known as the first time that astronauts were allowed to walk in space. On February 7, McNair's fellow astronauts Robert Stewart and Bruce McCandless became the first humans to fly "free" in space. Aided by special jet-propelled backpacks, the two men spent 12 hours "space walking" outside of *Challenger*.

Though McNair did not join his fellow crew members outside the spaceship, the rookie

A private man, McNair enjoyed spending time at home with his wife, Cheryl, and their son, Reginald. The couple's daughter, Joy Cheray, was born shortly after this picture was taken.

astronaut did conduct a series of important experiments on *Challenger*'s middeck. One of his assignments was to operate a remote sensory camera that recorded images of the earth as the shuttle sped above the planet's surface. McNair was also in charge of operating the shuttle's new, 50-foot remote manipulator arm, a mechanical attachment designed to recover damaged satellites in space. When operated by a skilled technician like

Ronald, the arm could be used to reach out and grab large pieces of equipment outside the ship. The equipment could then be stored in the shuttle's cargo bay and returned to earth for repairs.

McNair also had another, less serious, duty to perform. In packing his bags for the flight, he had included his saxophone along with his technical equipment to deal with the long hours of inactivity and boredom in space. With NASA's encouragement, he treated mission control to a lively musical performance while orbiting in the *Challenger*. Ronald's spirited performance earned him the distinction of being the first musician in the history of space travel. Finally on February 12, 1984, the shuttle finished its mission and landed safely at Cape Kennedy. After eight days in space and 27 orbits around the earth, McNair was now a full-fledged astronaut.

Back home in Lake City, South Carolina, the news of astronaut McNair's first successful spaceflight was a cause for pride. The city held a special, daylong celebration—including a parade, a fireworks display, and speeches by friends and city officials—to commemorate McNair's achievement. Black citizens and white citizens alike were eager to pay tribute to their hometown hero. In what McNair considered the greatest honor of all, the city renamed its main street, the section of U.S. Highway 52 that cut through the center of town, Ronald E. McNair Boulevard. In the town park, Ronald's astronaut boot prints were permanently embedded in a block of concrete. This was the same park that had once been off-limits to McNair and the city's other black residents.

Eventually, all the attention began to have a positive effect on McNair outside his work as a space technician. Previously known for his serious and shy personality, he now became one of the more popular astronauts. Once noted for his intense privacy about personal matters, he was now willing to talk openly about his experience as one of the few minority members of the astronaut corps. He was regularly called upon to speak at social functions and other public gatherings as a representative of NASA.

Whenever he spoke at schools and universities, McNair always made a point of inviting young students to his lectures, especially minority students. He felt that it was his responsibility to serve as a role model for those who might otherwise never have thought about pursuing a career in science. In his public speaking, McNair often referred to his own personal struggles on his way to becoming an astronaut. "The unknown is frightening," he explained to his listeners. "But you can only become a winner if you are willing to walk over the edge and dangle over it just a little bit." As an astronaut, McNair had learned that challenges and risks were a part of life. He believed that even the most underprivileged of children were capable of many great achievements—if they were encouraged to take risks and explore their potential. Some, he hoped, might even become astronauts.

A Kennedy Space Center official watches helplessly as the Challenger *disappears in a dense cloud of smoke. Onlookers around the world were shocked and saddened by the explosion that took the lives of the seven* Challenger *crew members.*

CHAPTER

6

A Hero
Remembered

NASA launched the space shuttle *Discovery* on September 29, 1988, more than two years after the accident that destroyed the *Challenger*. The first shuttle to launch since the tragedy, *Discovery* flew a near-flawless mission that helped put the U.S. space program back on its feet.

As a part of their mission, the *Discovery* crew launched the replacement for a satellite that had been destroyed on the failed *Challenger* mission. While in orbit, the crew members also read tributes to the brave astronauts who had died on the earlier mission. After two years of redesigning its *priorities* and capabilities, NASA was finally ready to continue with the space program.

The role of the astronaut would continue to be a highly visible one. Not many people are given the opportunity to fly into space. Those few who do become role models for the rest of society. Pioneers in the infant field of space travel, astronauts serve as an example to those on earth of how people working together, in spite of their differences, can achieve remarkable goals.

Ronald McNair took this responsibility seriously. Throughout his life, McNair's commitment to both excellence and equality helped close the gap between black people and white people. From his childhood sit-in at the Lake City Public Library to his mature achievements in the U.S. space program, McNair was a true pioneer.

MIT president Paul Gray once described McNair as a leader who used his own interests and enthusiasm to build "bridges between people."

"A black man who grew up in a segregated society," explained Gray, "Ron used his talents and teachings—in science, in religion, in the arts, in athletics—to form friendships and connections with many people from many races and cultures. In forming these bridges, he was able to retain and, indeed, to celebrate his own cultural identity."

When McNair spoke to young audiences, he often told the story of a courageous eagle who—because he had been raised by chickens—thought that he was a chicken. "The chickens had wings but could not fly," McNair explained to his listeners. "They lived together but didn't protect each other. Then, one day, the eagle saw a flock of eagles fly by. The young eagle felt a pride he had never experienced. He ran across the barnyard, flapped his wings, and left the chickens on the ground, soaring over the trees and mountaintop."

"Black students, minority students," McNair continued, "you're not chickens, you're eagles! You don't belong on the ground. Stretch your wings and fly to the sky!"

The most extensive marine salvage operation in history
was required to recover the remains of the wrecked
spacecraft from the ocean. Investigation of the fragments
revealed that faulty O-rings had led to the disaster.

Ronald McNair knew what encouragement could do for a young person. Those who followed his career could testify firsthand about the extraordinary impact he often had on youngsters everywhere. According to Colonel Charles Bolden, one of McNair's fellow astronauts, many young people were inspired by McNair's courageous example to enter the space program. "I see young men and women coming to MIT," explained Bolden, "and saying, 'I want to go where Ron McNair went. I want to go where Ron McNair dared. I want to go where Ron McNair chose to start his life taking risks.'"

There were many tributes to McNair after his death in the *Challenger* explosion. Back in Lake City, Carver High School was renamed Ronald E. McNair Junior High School, in memory of its most famous student. In December of 1986, MIT dedicated the Ronald E. McNair Building, a large structure that houses the university's Center for Space Research and part of its aeronautics and astronautics department. McNair's own hope for

In December 1986, MIT dedicated the Ronald E.
McNair Building, housing the university's Center for
Space Research. McNair's words were engraved in the
lobby: "My wish is that we would allow this planet to be
the beautiful oasis that she is, and allow ourselves to live
more in the peace that she generates."

the future is engraved in the building's cornerstone.

"My wish is that we would allow this planet to be the beautiful oasis that she is," said McNair, "and allow ourselves to live more in the peace that she generates." McNair's words came from the heart. A child of poverty and segregation, he knew firsthand the crippling effects that a hostile environment could have on a young person. Throughout his life, he dedicated himself to creating a world in which all people could one day realize their dreams.

"Say that he was an achiever," said Paul Gray during a special memorial service for McNair held at MIT. "Ron was not content with halfway measures, with average goals, with median achievements. . . . He stuck to his dreams, and he brought to each part of his life an indomitable spirit and a shining belief in his own capacity to succeed. He held the promise of future leadership for a nation that has too few heroes. Ron McNair is, was, a real live hero."

Further Reading

Asimov, Isaac. *Think About Space: Where Have We Been and Where Are We Going?* New York: Walker, 1989.

Bernstein, Joanne E., and Rose Blue. *Judith Resnik: Challenger Astronaut.* New York: Lodestar Books, 1990.

Billings, Charlene W. *Christa McAuliffe: Pioneer Space Teacher.* Hillside, NJ: Enslow, 1986.

Bond, Peter. *Heroes in Space: From Gagarin to Challenger.* New York: Blackwell, 1987.

Cohen, Daniel, and Susan Cohen. *Heroes of the Challenger.* New York: Archway, 1986.

Haskins, Jim, and Kathleen Benson. *Space Challenger: The Story of Guion Bluford.* Minneapolis: Carolrhoda Books, 1984.

Jones, Brian. *Space Exploration.* Milwaukee: Gareth Stevens Children's Books, 1990.

Naden, Corrine. *Ronald McNair: Astronaut.* New York: Chelsea House, 1991.

Glossary

aptitude   a natural ability or talent; quickness to learn

conventional   following accepted practice, customs, or taste

cosmonaut   an astronaut in the Soviet (now Russian) space program

efficiently   bringing about a desired result without waste of time, materials, or energy

engulf   to swallow up or cover completely

illuminate   to light up

jeopardize   to put in danger

minority   a group of people that differs, as in race, from the larger population

orbit   the path by which an object circles another object in space; to move along that path

postponement   putting off until a later time

74

predecessor one coming before, as in time, order, or rank

prejudice a strong feeling or opinion formed unfairly or without knowing all the facts; bias

priority coming before in time, order, or importance

probe a device used to send information from outer space back to earth

propel to cause to move forward or onward

racism a belief that one's own race is superior to another

ridicule to use words or actions intended to make fun of someone or something

satellite an object launched by a rocket intended to circle the earth, the moon, or another celestial body

scholarship a grant of money given to help a student continue his or her education

segregated separated and set apart from a main body or group, frequently on the basis of race

valedictorian the student with the highest rank in a graduating class

Chronology

1950   Born Ronald Erwin McNair on October 21, in Lake City, South Carolina

1961   Yuri Gagarin of the Soviet Union orbits the earth and becomes the first person in space

1967   McNair graduates as valedictorian from Carver High School

1969   The U.S. crew of the *Apollo 8* becomes the first to land on the moon

1971   McNair graduates magna cum laude from North Carolina Agricultural and Technical State University with a degree in physics; receives a scholarship from the Ford Foundation to attend Massachusetts Institute of Technology

1976   Receives doctorate in physics from MIT; marries Cheryl Moore on June 27

1978   Chosen by NASA to be a new recruit for the U.S. space program

1982 McNair's first child, Reginald, is born

1984 Second child, Joy Cheray, is born; McNair makes his first spaceflight aboard the *Challenger*

1986 Makes second journey into space and dies in the *Challenger* explosion on January 28

Index

Dena Shaw received a B.A. from the University of Wisconsin where she studied English literature and creative writing. She lives and writes in Madison, Wisconsin.

Picture Credits